Be You and Live Civil

By: Karen Civil

ISBN: **0692558934**

ISBN 13: **978-0692558935**

ACKNOWLEDGEMENTS

I cannot express enough thanks to my family for their continued support and encouragement: Mom, Dad, my brothers Mike & Jeff. My sister Charisse, Uncle Robinson, my niece & nephews; Carleigh Marie, Corey & Carter I love you more than words can describe.

Monique, Sable, Steve Carless, Amber Ravenel, Robin, CJ, Chris, Olori, Ming, Zenova, Rebecca, Angel, Tiffany, Stephanie Awekey, Janee, Leonard Brooks, Jason Davis, Angela Yee, Karen Miller, Teyana Taylor, Kiesha Reddy, Vanessa Anderson & Brian Miller - thank you for your support.

The completion of this project could not have been accomplished without the assistance of Youri Pascal, Ashley Taylor, Nicole McGloster, Ayanna Sinclair, Mike Boyce, James McMillian, Jonathan Taylor, Oz, Joilisa, India, Stephanie, Christian & The Haynes family.

Angie Martinez, FunkmasterFlex, Tat Wza, Duke Da God, Joie Manda, Mack Maine, Lil Wayne & Pusha T, thank you for taking a chance and giving me an opportunity.

My Angels: Cleavon Haynes, Joseph Miles III, Steven "A$AP Yams" Rodriguez

Finally, to everyone who inspired me throughout my journey and most importantly, made sure I never gave up on my dreams or myself, my heartfelt thanks.

Preface: Never Let Up

My muscles were shrieking. Putting one Nike Air Zoom Pegasus 31 in front of the other, I'd just finished running thirteen agonizing miles for Nike Women's Half Marathon San Francisco under the city's usual perfect-for-running skies. But even after a little over two and a half hours of pushing my entire body to its limits, my heart wouldn't let up. I just kept running.

Back when hip-hop heads all hailed Dipset as the greatest rap crew ever, Joseph Miles III and I were interning for Yandy Smith and Jim Jones at Diplomat Records. He commuted from Long Island, and I commuted from Elizabeth, New Jersey; he went to

LaSalle University while I put college on pause. But every day, as we sat in our cubicles next to one another, I naturally gravitated toward him because we had a connection and our purposes aligned. He was just different.

One of the seldom times I questioned God was when I visited Joseph in the hospital not long after we'd built a solid friendship. He graduated early and became super intern-turned-Dipskate-manager, but as quickly as he scratched the surface of success, he was diagnosed with Hodgkin's lymphoma. It was hard to grow with somebody, watch him achieve great things, and then sit by his bedside and cry. It was weird meeting his parents under those circumstances, seeing his twin brother Ken. It was all just very emotional.

I remember leaving the hospital that night and telling him that I'd see him tomorrow. The next morning, I received a call from his brother—"Joseph's gone."

I just couldn't stop screaming.

It's one thing to be aware that life is short, but it sometimes takes a heart-stopping tragic event to truly understand that nothing in life is promised except death. Joseph was a brilliant kid who was about to dominate the industry, and now he's no longer here. It's painful enough when a parent, or grandparent dies. But, when a young person dies, I would consider it to be a life that we can only wonder about: what positive impact could he or she have had? What medical cures could they have discovered? What person's life could they have made a difference in that they may have helped that person see the potential in themselves that no one else saw? These are things we will never know, but, whether young, or old, every death has a major impact.

As the poet John Donne said: "Every man's death diminishes me." And so are we all diminished when Joseph passed from this world. I admired Joe for his strengths, & loved him for his imperfections. In life, it's the possibility that keeps us going, not the guarantee.

So I keep on running. I happily finish the Nike Women's run every year in Joseph's honor to help benefit the Leukemia & Lymphoma Society (LLS) in their mission to find cures for blood cancers. I know that he's with me the whole time, —not just for the marathon, but also in life, pushing me to do things and to exceed my own expectations. So even when my mind is clouded and the pain riddles my body, I can't let up

in this race of life. I *have* to keep running. For Joseph.

CHAPTER 1

Understanding Yourself: The Power of Acceptance

I'm not for everybody, and I'm grateful for that.

My fifth-grade graduation from Lafayette Middle School was very amusing. Some parents came from work and wore professional clothing, and some came from home, wearing casual clothes. Well, my mom came in a blue ball gown as if she were going to the Emmys or the Oscars. When she walked in with such confidence, it was as if everything stopped. Everyone just looked. She had her hair in a French twist, her makeup was done to perfection, and she handed me a dozen roses in the midst of the teacher calling my name. She was so proud of me, just for the fact that I was accomplishing something. For her, it was major. That's when I knew my family was different, although I fought it even after that day.

Back then being Haitian wasn't cool. At least that's not what I thought while growing up. I would do anything possible to fit in, including hiding my parents' background, buying the latest fashion trends, begging my mom to listen to secular music, and so on. However, keeping up with what other kids my age deemed "cool" or "fun" became exhausting, overwhelming even. By the time I was in high school, I was the Haitian girl who wore all black and liked the Backstreet Boys (BSB). I wasn't in ESL like the majority of Haitian kids were, I wasn't sexually active, and I didn't sneak out to go to clubs. I didn't understand those activities, but I also didn't understand why those activities didn't interest me. So in 1997 I simply turned to the Internet.

Do you remember those CDs where you could download a free trial of AOL Internet? The dial-up sounds were like music to my ears, prepping the extra minutes I'd get to flit around the Internet (AOL Instant Messenger!), create whatever username I wanted, and not feel weighed down by the negative labels the world wanted me to subscribe to. At that time, the Internet was a new frontier for most people; this was pre-Google and way before Apple, the "it" company of design and function. Everything was a new experience, and I'd become so consumed with the uniqueness of this digital world that I'd taught myself how to build a website. Being the super BSB fan that I was at the time, I dedicated my first site to their fans, and later, around 2002, I created a similar "fan site" for actor J. D. Williams through Yahoo. The kids who visited and interacted on these cult-like e-platforms were creators of other fan clubs, just like me. It was dope to watch us all rally people together who had similar interests. Discovering that there was this whole other world I could connect to and share my true interests with, was one of the first steps in acquiring my true sense of self. The digital space became my safe haven. I wasn't weird; I was unique. And like my mother, I became proud to stand out from others. My differences would soon become one of my most important strengths.

***

Accepting yourself is an everyday, evolving thing. It doesn't happen overnight. It's a small seed inside you that blooms over time with every life lesson. It's true: as you grow older, you grow wiser—and not just about what's around you but about who you are at your core. We're all created with unique personalities and forms, even though at times we slam differences instead of celebrating them. So the first step to living in your purpose is to identify what sets you apart, as opposed to looking at what other people are doing and figuring out why you're not like them. Only heartache and poor choices stem from that type of behavior. Trust me, we all slip up and become distracted by other people's success stories, and it doesn't help that our generation of oversharing—with Instagram, Twitter, Facebook, Snapchat, and so on—encourages that type of behavior. When I started to discover my passions, I thought I needed to follow a certain blueprint and be like the next person, but when that didn't work for me, I branched out, accepted who I was, and found my footing in the digital world, which blossomed into cultivating my own community of people both on and offline.

Now I'm at a point where I'm content. I found my strength within and in those whom I love most, which allows me to make the decisions that truly cater to and draw into my life the energy I want from the universe. Not a lot of people have the courage to leave their hometowns to explore the world and figure out whom they are. Finding that inner courage to pursue your dreams and to tackle all the obstacles thrown at you is where it starts. That's how you gain mental strength. At my core, if any choice I decide to make doesn't work out, I can still feel completely anchored in my own confidence, control the room, and beam with pride.

Here are four steps you can take to understand yourself.

Stop All Negative Self-Talk and Cut Out Negative People

How can you hear your own positive voice when it's constantly drowned out by the negative talk of others or even your own negative self-talk? It's time to cut it out! Ignore those who speak ill to or about you and those who enable you to be self-deprecating. If it doesn't make you happy, you can't afford it. Your energy is on a strict budget. Once you've refreshed your phone contacts, you'll have a support system that reinforces the acceptance and understanding of yourself.

Find Your Community

So you've found your inner circle? Great! Now go bigger! Find a wider community that shares your interests and supports who you are and who you want to become on a larger scale. Do you enjoy running? Join a running club. Do you love helping others? Volunteer at a hospital or homeless shelter on weekends. Got a thing for gardening? Start a community garden. Just find ways to express your interests and get in sync with what you love and others that love it too.

Spend Time with Yourself

Spend time with yourself, cultivating your ideas and passion: Is this really what I want to do? If I make a dollar from it, will I be happy? If I don't make a dollar from it, will I be happy? I could be living on the street doing this; would I be OK with that?

Celebrate Your Strengths & What You Love About Yourself

Look yourself in the mirror and visualize the life you want to set forth for yourself.

Be kind to yourself. Accepting yourself starts with taking care of *you* with the best kind of TLC.

CHAPTER 2

Self-Motivation: The American Hustle

Are you willing to work for it or wait for it?

"Why didn't you come?" It was a common question I'd ask my dad growing up. On some of the happiest days of my life, I was always heartbroken when I looked around and my dad wasn't there. I'll never forget what he said to me one time I asked: "I wanted to be there, but you like this house, right? You like having certain things? I have to work for these things."

You see, it doesn't get any more mediocre than where I grew up in Elizabeth, New Jersey. That stretch of land on the tri-state map is nothing like being born in a full-of-life, bustling city like New York or Los Angeles, where the slightest whiff of air makes you want to work harder. In Elizabeth, excelling isn't championed, and few things are certain: first comes child, then comes a standard nine-to-five job, and then you live off the system and go on about your life. Those limited options were an unspoken criteria for a normal life, not an extraordinary one. And the community certainly didn't support you in becoming an excellent individual. Don't get me wrong—that boxed-in lifestyle is comfortable for some people. However, for me, I refused to become what my environment mapped out for me. I imagined creating a life that not only I, but also my hardworking immigrant parents, could be proud of. And I knew I had to work for it.

Realizing that I inherited my father's exact work ethic, I set out to reach new, unimaginable heights by taking the reins of my own destiny. The first step was finding my footing in an industry I've adored since I was a young pre-teen attending live tapings of BET's 106 & Park countdown show.

I remember being 20 years old, hanging out in my room, listening to Hot 97 FM for hours when one day Angie Martinez comes over the airwaves and revealed that she was holding a contest to find her new apprentice. The contest, which was called Apprentice II, would give a young man or woman an opportunity to learn the ins and outs of the industry. I remember thinking this was it? This was my chance to finally get my foot in the door.

Just my luck, it was the final day to enter the contest. As I hear Angie announce the submission email, I quickly ran to my computer desk. I knew exactly what I needed to do. This wasn't a time to try to oversell myself or pretend to be someone I'm not. I just had to write from the heart — and that's what I did. I'm typing away, explaining to Angie Martinez that all I'm asking for is an opportunity, for someone to believe in me and give me a chance to be great.

I sent off the email and after a few days I receive a response from Mike, Angie Martinez's intern. He tells me that Angie liked my email and wanted me to come down to the Hot 97's studios. I couldn't believe it. I took that first step, spilled my heart out and it was that easy. I was going to be working with Angie Martinez in New York City!

On the day I was to meet with Angie, I didn't tell my mom where I was going. Leaving Elizabeth, for us, was a big deal. Going to NYC was a luxury, something we only did on holidays or special occasions. This would be the first time I ever ventured into the city alone. Not only that, this was the very first time I had ever taken the train alone. I only had $14.00 in my pocket, barely enough to take the NJ Transit to Penn Station, but when I finally got to New York I head down to Hot 97 to embark on my first day as Angie Martinez's apprentice.

When I arrived I remember seeing a room full of people who apparently had also been picked by Angie. Once I got over the fact that I was not the sole winner, but that I am still competing, I knew that shy, timid Karen would have to boss up and make this moment count. There I was, standing within arm's reach of my dreams. Once I got a small glimpse of what my life could be, I knew there was no turning back.

So day after day, I would go to work for Angie. I would do everything right. I would get coffee, answer the hotline calls, the tasks got crazier and crazier, but whatever I had to do I would give 110%, and with every day another one of my competitors was eliminated. It came to a point where there were only three of us standing. Here I was, beginning the newest chapter in my life. I was about to win the Apprentice II contest. In my mind, I had the job but unfortunately I didn't win. Instead, I went back home to Elizabeth, New Jersey.

I didn't take this as my cue to give up. Determined to make it, I would call into Funkmaster Flex's hotline daily, asking for a shot to intern for him. One day, as I placed my routine call to Funk Flex, the associate producer of the show, Tat Wza, answers the phone. He tells me that during my time competing in Angie Martinez's contest, I caught Flex's attention. He said that Flex noticed how hard I was working and would like to offer me a position interning for his radio show. My time had arrived. All of my work, albeit for someone else, had paid off.

No matter the hits or misses I've experienced in my career, the fact that my parents sacrificed a lot to make a better life for my brother and I is why I've taken "Believe in yourself like you believe in God" as a personal mantra. Sure, the balancing act between work and pleasure can be difficult, but for now I've divided my energy so that a lot of it is dedicated to my work.

As of last year, I've stepped into the waters of dedicating 24/7 of my time to my company. There is no on-and-off switch for what I need to handle when it comes to business. It's my passion and my life, and I continuously make sacrifices now for a better tomorrow. Don't get this confused with "Team No Sleep," though; the only way for your body and mind to be fully rejuvenated is to rest. The key to pushing yourself to excel, isn't lack of sleep, but to properly manage your time while you're awake.

However, self-motivation coupled with never playing it safe is what really projects your success into the next stratosphere. President of the Robot Company, Paul Rivera once told me, "Karen, there are people who are born to follow and those who are born to lead. Why are you in line?"

It's that type of encouraging sentiments that pushed me to launch Always Civil Enterprise, my digital and marketing company. Former employees have now become clients of the business.

That's such a major confirmation that trusting who I am and constantly motivating myself has steadily kept me on the right path. Sure, it's scary, but that fear does not outweigh my determination to continuously lead my life with my career.

Life is an endless cycle of work and working harder as your success grows. Now is the time to cut the whining and complaining. Figure out what you want, and then develop a plan. Figure out a way to make up for lost time; find the most direct path to your goals. Actions speak louder than words, so show the world what you've got. Be about your business(es), and find room for improvement. There is no room in your life for fear and faith. Each day you MUST decide which one gets to stay.

Here are three affirmations to repeat daily that will constantly push you forward:

- **If I focus on the road in front of me and on moving forward, then I can safely speed past the fears and criticisms that are nearby.**

- **I will not be focused on anyone's success but my own. No matter how appealing their lives may seem, their successes do not outshine my own.**

- **I am fearless in the pursuit of what sets my soul on fire.**

Your motivation must come from within, and the intensity of that motivation is determined by how badly you want to perform well.

CHAPTER 3

Fill Up on Your Happy: Emotional Control and a

Positive, Realistic Attitude

You are not going to be able to do or deal with everything.

I was ready to die. My gut-wrenching sobs were ringing through my one-bedroom apartment by the time my eyes found the bottle of Percocet sitting on the table. The person I put all this time and effort into decided he no longer was interested in a relationship with me and had used me to help benefit his career. Around the same time, I'd lost my job working with Dipset, and I was fed up with feeling like I didn't have control over my life. I was losing the relationship and the career I'd worked hard to build and frankly, I just wanted to give up.

My friend Stephanie was on the phone, giving me her usual reassuring spiel about how everything would be all right, but the darkness of emotional turmoil clouded any optimism. Instead of finding solace in her words, I chucked the cordless phone against the wall and swallowed close to ten pills.

I didn't leave a note.

I just wanted somebody to find me.

I wanted to be rescued from life and everything about it but God saw fit to force me to deal with reality and face the issues that led me to suicide, and I woke up the next day.

Nowadays, when I look around, I take inventory

of the family and friends that I was about to throw away because life was getting hard. I was getting ready to waste my talent, my passion, and my purpose because I was heartbroken. I was making the mistake of choosing a permanent solution over a temporary situation. Taking my life would have only transferred the pain I was feeling onto all the ones who loved me. I wouldn't have had the chance to see my niece go to the first grade or to watch videos of my nephew making his first touchdown. I had to realize my current situation was *not* my final destination.

Because of that dark hour when God refused to give up on me, when I was so unsure of my purpose, I thank him every day by never giving up on myself. Although I'm not the most religious person in the world, I believe in a higher, more divine power than myself. That higher power saw fit to intervene when I had given up on myself and that higher power remained with me as I took a leap of faith, packed up my Nissan, and left the comforts of New Jersey for the big city life of Los Angeles.

Getting in tune with positive energies through meditation and yoga is also an important part of my lifestyle now. So even though I'm what you would call a workaholic, I take breaks throughout the year to reconnect with my spiritual beliefs and to help myself regain mental strength and clarity.

Mike and I were raised Christian—Baptist for a few years and Jehovah's Witness for a short period of time after that. When I got older, I finally realized that I needed to buckle down and find understanding to the many unanswered questions I had about life, divine power, and spiritual vibrations. So I started attending a non-denominational church after my suicide attempt. That helped me find a lot of balance and understanding of who I am. It helped me steady my emotions without the use of drugs. And it felt so, so good.

Nowadays, at the end of the year, I count my blessings with my Live Civil Blessings Jar. Every year leading up to the New Year, we tend to remember every horrible misfortune that we've come across, but this Blessings Jar is my way of remembering the light that shines in my life every day. Throughout the year, whenever something good happens in my life, whether big or small, I write it down on a piece of paper and place it into my Blessings Jar. Whether I've landed a new client, reached a goal I've set for myself, or simply celebrated a birthday with those I love most, I take time to acknowledge the things in life that are not promised. At the end of each year, I empty the jar and count my blessings, which helps me enter a new calendar year with a positive outlook and realistic view of my life. After that, I fill up on my happy, as I call it, by taking a trip to Disneyland. I've done it for the last four years: get a hug from Minnie Mouse, buy a Mickey balloon, eat some funnel cake, and end the day at the spa afterwards. When I get back home, I sage my house and light my candle. That's how I kick-start my year and maintain the positive energy throughout.

Even on the Bad Days, Life Is Good

Not too long ago, I had a feeling that something in my life was falling apart. I couldn't put my finger on it or even articulate it effectively, but I trusted that no day is so bad that things will never be good again. There's a misconception that a positive outlook is a state of constant delusion—that's not true. Life is built to throw adversity at you, even when you're at your lowest. But what's beautiful is that you can feel dark emotions and not succumb to them, knowing that it's just a phase. As an exercise, when things aren't going your way, remind yourself that the goal is to progress not regress.

Fill Up on Your Happy

Here's how you can create your own Blessings Jar:

- Make it fun and colorful, and add a bunch of stuff that reflects your personality.

- Once you've designed your jar, place a notepad and a pen inside the jar, so that every time something great happens to you, you can write it down and stick it in the jar.

- At the end of the year, dump the notes out and spend time looking back on your blessings!

By focusing on your strengths, you gain confidence and inspiration from them, creating a positive attitude toward life as a whole.

CHAPTER 4

Living Civil

Knowing your worth is more important than letting

someone define your value.

Being in Haiti for the first time is a memory I barely remember because I was so young when I went there with my family. My memories consist of the pictures my mom has of my brother and me in her living room. We were around four or five at the time so going back to Haiti was definitely long overdue.

I had so many mixed emotions about what would happen. We heard the stories of family members being kidnapped and ransomed for money, getting robbed, or worse -- never returning home. The organization I traveled with for my birthday knew of all my hesitations and made sure that my 30th birthday in Haiti was a remarkable one.

For this trip I traveled with my camera guy, Amil, and my brand manager, Ashley Taylor. Before we departed I told them I said a prayer for our safe return home and I promised that I would protect their lives as if they were my own.

The day finally arrived for us to travel. Spending my birthday in Haiti was very different from my normal travels. I would usually spend it on some tropical island getting a nice tan and counting my blessings. This year it was bigger than me. I wanted to celebrate this milestone by doing something bigger than me, building and creating my first ever Live Civil Playground for the kids in Haiti. I always knew how important a playground was to me growing up and how it contributed to my growth and personality. I wanted to create the same opportunity for the less fortunate children who deserved to have the same.

When we stepped off the plane in Haiti we were greeted with local island music and warm smiles. Our trip organizer met us, gave us kisses and escorted us right away to a private diplomat area where they took care of our passports, luggage and other details. While we were there we just sat and talked about what was to be expected.

As we headed outside, we saw cop cars and three black SUVs. I asked if the president was nearby. They replied, "No, this was for you." I was shocked. I knew they said we would have security detail, but I had no idea that we would travel around Haiti like I was

First Lady Michelle Obama. We weaved through traffic, headlights and sirens blaring for folks to move out of our way. I felt slightly guilty that I was getting all of this special treatment. I wondered if I even deserved it.

We checked in to our hotel and found ourselves spending day one in Haiti relaxing and preparing ourselves for tomorrow's big day. I wanted to make sure that while in Haiti I was there that I took some time to support the local small businesses so we visited some of those local shops and bought hand- crafted heart rocks and little statues to give as gifts for family and friends back home. I must have spent over $200, but it was definitely well worth it.

Later that day we decided to visit the playground Donna Karen built in one of Haiti's slums, on the outskirts of Port-au-Prince. I wanted to take this opportunity to get last minute ideas for creating my own Live Civil playground. The day was clear and warm, and the weather perfect for reflecting quietly for a moment before things got too hectic the next day. While I was looking around, a local boy approached the gate, and out of curiosity I walked through the bushes over to him.

"Hey, what are you doing here?" I asked.

"Well, I saw the car, and I thought it was someone important," he said, explaining that he'd walked more than a mile to find out who I was. "I saw you standing there, and I just wanted to say hello."

We talked without reservations. He wasn't a poor, young local, and I wasn't in his country building a playground he may never get to experience. We weren't strangers—just two people trading life stories and connecting. We ended the chat with me passing him some fruit and money he could take back to his family. And as he departed, taking that mile walk back to his reality, I realized his thirst for conversation, his curiosity, would stick with me forever.

I slept peacefully that night and waking up the next morning felt like a dream. The big day had come. It was November 8th, my 30th birthday. My mind raced as I worried about what to expect. Would the kids like me? Was I doing the right thing? Every moment of concern came over me and I had to calm myself and remember that I was doing this for the kids.

The dress I chose to wear was a heritage print dress by Haitian fashion designer, Stella Jean. I looked myself in the mirror and gave myself a final pep talk before leaving the hotel. "You are thirty. You've accomplished so much and this is the first step to creating a legacy that will live on. Your family is proud, you are proud, and you are becoming the woman you are meant to be."

As we headed to the school, the smile on my face was one I'll never forget. All my fears and worries went away. As the kids hugged and embraced me, I knew this would be the best birthday I'd ever had.

We planted the first tree, held the park ceremony and check donation ceremony, and then after all the business stuff was done, it was fun time with the kids. From popcorn and ice cream, to the soccer balls I had brought, we spent the rest of the afternoon smiling, laughing and just having fun. It was such a surreal feeling to watch their worries fade away with each passing moment.

I spent the final day in Haiti at a resort beach reminiscing about the day before and how incredible it was. I was filled with joy as I thought about all of the new friends I had made and the happiness on the kids' faces. I was going home renewed, accomplished and in high spirits.

The gift of giving was my 30th birthday.

Not too many people actually imprint themselves on my life forever. For the most part, I stick to my small circle of loved ones, unless of course I'm forced to be in a social setting for work. But traipsing around the United States for the Live Civil Tour has ripped me from my comfort zone in terms of connecting with people. I've found myself in places and cities I've never visited before, understanding new perspectives, hearing new ideas, and learning new things. People praise international trips—they're awesome, don't get me wrong—but the amount of culture one can garner in your own backyard is profound. It's one thing for someone to tweet it to you or mention it to you in a comment, but it's another thing for people to feel so comfortable in person to talk to you about their passions and future plans. Hearing stories from the people I've met, seeing how they chase their dreams despite their environments or the obstacles they face, are some of the most refreshing things to experience.

Let's not forget: I went from being an awkward kid from Jersey to starting a music blog that's now grown into a larger initiative and is actually making a difference in people's lives. It's a testament to the possibilities of this life and how life should be lived: live it in your purpose and to the fullest—each and every moment.

You see, everyone desires recognition, whether it's in the form of an award or a prize or something that confirms your reasons for outworking others. Although your reward may be money, there are non-monetary accolades that are more fulfilling than any check anyone can cut.

I'm not just connecting with beautiful spirits across the globe; I'm actually living! I love outdoor activities. I surf, I go ATVing, and I like to play volleyball. I don't live my entire life on the Internet, even though that's where I started. My whole world has opened up, and I've become a citizen of it. My trophies are not only rooted in how I live my life each day, but they are also in the giveback. I want to continuously create guidelines for people to follow on their paths to success, to give back to the communities that have given to me, and to give back to the young women who may not have a voice. I believe God continues to keep me here to inspire the next person to grow.

Honestly, my life has come full circle in so many ways that I'm constantly reminded that I'm on the right path.

When my dear friend A$AP Yams passed away in January 2015, I was heartbroken. I'll never forget this day; I was in Atlanta on my Live Civil Tour. I woke up that morning, as I normally do, and hopped on social media to see what today's argument, conversation or breaking news story was. I saw my timeline filled with a bunch of "RIP A$AP YAMS" tweets and I said to myself, "Here goes Twitter trying to kill someone off again." I paid it no mind. I went over to read some of the comments on my Instagram page and this one comment stood out. It read, "Yams died, Karen."

My eyes began to water and it's like the hotel room had no air. My body was stiff and heavy. I just kept looking at the comment thinking to myself, "No way." I called a mutual friend of ours, and the answered the phone crying. He said, "Yeah, Yams is gone, Karen," and began sobbing heavily into the phone.

Here I was, the day of my first Atlanta speaking engagement, a complete mess. My hair and makeup people arrived and I found myself breaking down. My brand manager Ashley was with me, assuring me that if this was something I emotionally couldn't do, it was okay to cancel. I replayed our last conversation over and over. I couldn't figure out how a kid with so much potential could no longer be here. I didn't want to accept reality.

I got up and sat on the side of the bed, thinking of what Yams would want me to do. I dried my eyes, and reminded myself that there were more than two hundred people waiting for me to share my story, and today I was going to share the story of A$AP Yams, this kid who went from being an intern to creating a legacy within the hip-hop community.

I met Yams via the Internet. I knew him as Stevie and he was part of the Juelz.com message board. One day he stopped by the store owned by rapper Juelz Santana and his mother, Santana's Town, on 153rd Street in Harlem. He definitely wasn't what I expected. He wore big baggy clothes, and braids. He kind of reminded me of a chubby version of rapper Paul Wall. We would have light conversations about music here and there until one day he asked me to help get him an internship. At this time I was an A&R admin for Duke Da God, the A&R representative for Diplomat Records. We always needed help packing CDs and doing odd jobs, so I said why not? Why not hire someone who loves the group so much? At least I knew he would go above and beyond for his job.

I have to admit, at times Stevie's slick mouth and opinionated thoughts would become annoying, but he was one of the fastest CD packing interns we had. Unlike the rest of the interns, Stevie would come in and talk about his future, how he made beats, and how he was going to become a rapper one day. I liked that about him. He had a determination; this look in his eye. It's like he could predict his future and that he would someday become successful. He just was waiting for it to happen.

On this particular day, Dipset had just dropped a collection tape. We were sitting around the office eating a pizza when Stevie asked me how he should go about building his brand. I explained to him that brand building boils down to people knowing about your company before you even walk in the door. You have to create something and have something that you feel is needed, then represent it so hard that no one can deny your brand's presence. I remember him saying "Okay, that's what's up." Not thinking he took what I said seriously, I just went back to taking CD orders.

It was about a week later that Stevie came in with this big "A$AP" tattoo on his arm and a purple CD he called "A$AP Productions." He dropped the CD on my desk, rolled up his sleeve and showed me his tattoo. He said, "This is "A$AP," my brand." I gave him the biggest smirk. I couldn't believe he took what I said to heart.

Stevie would walk the floors of the Atlantic Records office giving a CD containing his beats to A&R people or anyone who would take it. Usually we would discourage soliciting but there was something about Stevie that meant business. He interned for almost two years before venturing off on his own and though we lost contact for a few years, I always would keep an eye on him and watch his growth. Then one day, to my surprise, he emailed me a video by his artist, A$AP Rocky. It was A$AP Rocky's very first video. I remember the email word for word. It read, "What up, this Stevie from Riverdale lol. I told you I had some shit. You gotta post this before it got hot, ya feel me? This about to be it. So look out, cause we about to take over, pls love you, KC!" His email had so much braggadocio that I just felt inclined to post the video of this A$AP Rocky kid on KarenCivil.com. I posted it and there he was in all his glory.

We remained in contact through the last few years and he was definitely right about A$AP Rocky.

He did blow up and I was definitely an A$AP Rocky fan. It was great to see Stevie at this place of success.

I'll never forget our last conversation. It was just before Christmas. I called him randomly to check on him because I heard he attended rehab but I wasn't sure of the seriousness of it. He answered the phone in high spirits, adding his slick jokes in there. We touched on our first ever conversation about building his brand and how he never put a limit on his success. I told him how proud I was of him and we talked about his future plans. I told him I was writing this book and that I was going to include him in some way. We left our phone conversation on a high note and promised to catch up when he got to Los Angeles.

I find myself revisiting our emails and text messages. I haven't been able to delete his number from my phone, hoping one day it'll ring again. I remember our countless conversations; he wanted to be an A&R, have an artist, have a rap group—and he reached a lot of his goals. Before he left, he touched a lot of people. I'm just happy that I was able to see his growth, and to see him live out the things he discussed very early on when he was an intern. It's crazy because he possessed so much potential, and he did so many great things in the nine years he was in this business.

The hip-hop community lost such a great individual, and I continue to see Stevie, as someone who chased his dreams, never took "no" for an answer, and created such an inspiring legacy in a short time.

The impact Stevie had on me is one I want to have on other young people who are interested in following their dreams but are reluctant to do so. My life has had its twists and turns, but ultimately every moment, including the bad, has helped mold me into the individual I am today. Never succumbing to negativity or giving up on the dreams that I had for myself, is a huge reason I'm here, able to share my story with you. I've dealt with countless disappointment, pill addiction, and the death of some incredible people, but giving up will never be an option.

To the person reading this, I want you to know that life is a roller coaster. It will have its ups and downs. There will be days you don't want to get out of bed, and it all feels hopeless. Just know that I've been in that position, too, and it's up to you to put on that invisible cape and become your own superhero. I've gone from almost being in the poor house, to speaking at the White House. Never putting a time limit on the success I saw for myself. All things are possible with patience and hard work. Believe in yourself, your vision and your purpose.

Daily Affirmations:

- I am the architect of my life; I build its foundation and choose its contents.

- Today, I am brimming with energy and overflowing with joy.

- My body is healthy; my mind is brilliant; my soul is tranquil.

- I am superior to negative thoughts and low actions.

- I have been given endless talents which I begin to utilize today.

- I possess the qualities needed to be extremely successful.

- My business will grow, expand, and thrive

- Creative energy surges through me and leads me to new and brilliant ideas.

- I deserve to be employed and paid well for my time, efforts, and ideas.

- My thoughts are filled with positivity and my life is plentiful with prosperity.

- Today, I abandon my old habits and take up new, more positive ones.

- I acknowledge my own self-worth; my confidence is soaring.

- I am a powerhouse; I am indestructible.

Things To Focus On:

Task That'll Help Me Grow:

Short Term Goals:

Long Term Goals:

Business Ideas:

Places To Travel: